The Bride
and the Slide

Kelly Doudna

Consulting Editor, Diane Craig, M.A./Reading Specialist

Published by ABDO Publishing Company, 4940 Viking Drive, Edina, Minnesota 55435.

Printed in the United States.

Credits
Edited by: Pam Price
Curriculum Coordinator: Nancy Tuminelly
Cover and Interior Design and Production: Mighty Media
Photo Credits: AbleStock, Hemera

Library of Congress Cataloging-in-Publication Data

Doudna, Kelly, 1963-
    The bride and the slide / Kelly Doudna.
        p. cm. -- (First rhymes)
    Includes index.
    ISBN 1-59679-455-0 (hardcover)
    ISBN 1-59679-456-9 (paperback)
        1. English language--Rhyme--Juvenile literature. I. Title. II. Series.

PE1517.D626 2006
808.1--dc22
                                                                      2005048048

SandCastle™ books are created by a professional team of educators, reading specialists, and content developers around five essential components that include phonemic awareness, phonics, vocabulary, text comprehension, and fluency. All books are written, reviewed, and leveled for guided reading and early intervention reading, and designed for use in shared, guided, and independent reading and writing activities to support a balanced approach to literacy instruction.

Let Us Know

After reading the book, SandCastle would like you to tell us your stories about reading. What is your favorite page? Was there something hard that you needed help with? Share the ups and downs of learning to read. We want to hear from you! To get posted on the ABDO Publishing Company Web site, send us e-mail at:

sandcastle@abdopub.com

SandCastle Level: Beginning

bride
ride

side

slide
wide

She is a .

She likes to  .

This is the .

See the .

This is .

The bride is happy.

Deb can ride
on the horse.

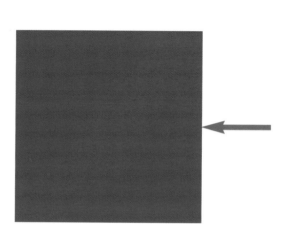

The side is flat.

The slide is yellow.

It is a wide river.

The Bride
and the Slide

Brenda is a bride.

Brenda the bride
stands beside
a river that is wide.

Brenda the bride
is on the wrong side
of the river that is wide.

20

Brenda the bride
sees a magic slide
over the river
that is wide.

"I'll take the slide
to the other side,"
says Brenda the bride.